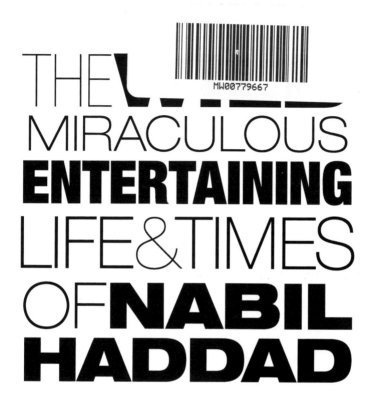

THE MIRACULOUS ENTERTAINING LIFE&TIMES OF NABIL HADDAD

BY NABIL HADDAD
WITH ALEX HOFFMAN

Louisburg Press
PO Box 4
Cleveland, MO 64734
Printed in the United States of America
IBSN: 978-0692509883

TABLE OF CONTENTS

FORWARD

Nabil is a born story teller.
Don't ask me how many times over the 50
plus years of our marriage I have heard these
stories – these and more. He has told them
in social gatherings of all kinds, in talks to
groups of all kinds, at family gatherings of
all kinds. Now he has told them to you in this
book.

They are wild and wonderful and entertaining
stories. No need to read them in order. You
might want to read the one called *Arrested in
Baghdad* first.

Thanks to writer Alex Hoffman for helping
us get them written down. Thanks to graphic
designer Ted Stone for the cover.

Peggy Haddad
August 2015

EARLY LIFE IN
THE MIDDLE EAST

MY DAD THE ORPHAN

World War I made my dad an orphan. His
father, Joseph, joined the Palestinian Brigade
to help the British drive the Turks out of
Palestine. He died in the war, leaving my
grandmother in Jerusalem with six children,
no money, and no income. She found a place
for them to live in the guard room above St.
Stephen's Gate.

She washed clothes, she cleaned houses, she
did whatever she had to do to support them.
My father, Abraham, was one of those kids.
She couldn't really take care of them all, so
keeping John the oldest with her, she sent the
others to live with relatives. My father, who
was eight years old at the time, was sent to
another town 30 miles from Jerusalem to stay
with her brother. So my father walked to that
town, all alone, eating grapes and figs along
the way. When you eat figs and touch your
eyes, it can cause an allergic reaction that

makes your eyes weep and close up. When he arrived at his uncle's house and knocked, his cousin came to open the door for him. His uncle said from inside the house, "Who's there?"

"It's Abraham, Joseph's son."

"What does he want? We can't have him here."

"He's an orphan and the kid can hardly see. We can't send him away!"

So she brought him in, cleaned him up, and took care of him. He stayed there for some time, working with his uncle who was a blacksmith.

Later he went to a Red Cross orphanage, and so did his younger sister, Martha.

MY DAD FINDS A JOB

When my father was a young man, the Iraq Petroleum Company in Haifa was looking for employees. He and his brother, John, applied for job but neither one was hired – they had no experience. My father kept going to the employment office every single day, sitting on the bench. Someone would say to him, "Listen, Abraham, we hired everybody. We don't need anyone else."

"Yeah, but I don't have a job," he said, "so I might as well sit here in case something comes up."

He went there seven straight days, the first one in and the last one out. Finally, on the eighth day, the man in charge of hiring called to him and said, "Abraham, today we have two openings. One is mail clerk and the other one is to be a driver who will go in a caravan to Kirkuk, Iraq."

My father asked, "Which job pays more?"

"The driver."

"I'll take that job," he said.

There was one problem though -- he had never driven before! So he and his older brother rented a Model T Ford so he could learn to drive. All night long he drove that car all around the town and the next day was on his way to Kirkuk.

When my father got that job, he worked for that company for 30 years, retiring as the head of the shipping and receiving department. This story gave me the motivation to be persistent when I was looking for a job.

MY DAD THE GAMBLER

In January 1938, Abraham Haddad was a devoted husband and the father of a young daughter. He had a vice, however — he loved to gamble. One cold, dreary night, he lost his entire paycheck and was so upset and depressed that he wanted to kill himself. He didn't want to have to tell his wife that she couldn't pay her bills. How would she feed the family if the shops wouldn't extend her more credit?

He approached the edge of the river. In his billfold was a single English pound. He threw the billfold on the street, thinking that maybe a poor street sweeper would find it and someone would be happy because of his death.

Suddenly a voice spoke to him. "Abraham, do not kill yourself. Your wife is pregnant with a son, and I want you to call him Nabil."

He picked up his billfold, headed for home, and woke up my mother to tell her she was pregnant and would have a boy. She began to argue with him.

"I'd know if I was pregnant!" she screamed. "You lost your money, didn't you?"

"Yes," my father said to her and promised he wouldn't gamble again.

That whole month was very difficult for my mother, who had to go to buy food on credit from the people she hadn't been able to pay.

I was born October 18, 1938, and was named Nabil, which means "noble" in Arabic. I was born in Haifa, which in those days was Palestine.

MY DAD THE BOXER

When he lived in Amman, Jordan, my father used to box and was so good that he was a champion boxer for six consecutive years in the Middle East. In those days, you didn't have different weight classes -- you just went in there and fought. My dad's weight was just average, but he had a long reach, and he won every single fight.

King Abdullah, the great grandfather of the current king of Jordan, Abdullah II, would sit in the front row for my dad's fights. In those days, according to the rules back then, if the opponent crouched down with his hands in front of his face you weren't supposed to hit him anymore. This guy my dad was fighting one time, an African champion, kept doing that. Finally King Abdullah got sick of it, gave my dad a look and a wink, and overruling the referee, said, "Hit him!" My dad knocked that guy out cold.

When he was the champion for the sixth straight time, King Abdullah hired my father to train his two sons, Talal and Naif. My dad used to go to the palace and train them both in self-defense and boxing.

King Abdullah loved my dad and my aunt Martha. She handled all the wardrobe for the women in the royal family, even traveling to London and Paris to buy clothes for them. My aunt and my dad were often invited to parties at the palace.

One night my dad rolled his Model T Ford when he was out celebrating a defense of his title. He broke two ribs, but he didn't quit boxing. Holding one arm to his side to protect his broken ribs, he just boxed with one hand, and he still won!

Years later when I was 4 or 5 years old, my dad would get me up every morning to make me run around the train station parking lot, hoping to make me a boxer. All that running did give me endurance for playing soccer.

As a boxer, my father was always very protective of his children. There was a bully who lived on the third floor of our building who was told repeatedly to quit messing with me and my sister. This guy was always pushing my sister as we were walking home from school. My dad saw this one day and went to him and slapped him. He went home crying and told his dad and his uncles that my dad had hit him. His dad and one of his uncles came down to the street and said to my dad, "Hey, why don't you pick on someone your own size?"

My dad said, "Come on," and the fight was on.

At that time, our uncle was painting our apartment, and I went running to him. "Uncle! There's two guys fighting my dad!" He said, "Don't worry. He'll take care of them."

Then another of the bully's uncles came down and joined in. Now it was three against one. Before it was over, my dad had knocked the hell out of all of them. My dad taught me that if you have to get in a fight, hit first. And I did that a couple times.

I LEARN A LIFE LESSON

When I was about 15 or 16, my friends and I loved movies, especially Audie Murphy movies.

One day when we were leaving to go to the movies, my dad said, "What are you doing after the movie?" That would be around 2:30 in the afternoon.

"Nothing," I said.

"Do you want to meet me at the Club to shoot pool?"

"Sure."

So I went to the movies with my friends. It turned out that there was another Audie Murphy movie at 2:30 in a different part of town. Of course, I wanted to go with them to see it. In those days, the 1950's, we had no telephones, and I had no way to get a message to my dad. But I thought, well, my dad is an executive, and he'll have a lot of people who'd love to shoot pool with him. So I went ahead with my friends to the other movie.

I got home about 6:00, and my dad wasn't home yet. My mother said, "I thought you were going to meet him and shoot pool."

"I was, but I went to the movies instead."

We waited and waited, and my dad didn't show up. Long after dark, around 9:30 or 10:00, I started walking toward the Club. There was no bingo that night, no tennis tournament, no dance, so I couldn't figure out what my dad would be doing. Surely he wouldn't still be shooting pool.

I pulled open the door, and who's there sitting in the lobby all by himself but my dad, his only company the two janitors cleaning the floor. My dad looked up and greeted me cheerfully with a smile. "Hi, son! I knew you'd come. What took you so long? " I always wished he had yelled at me rather than heaping coals on my head by being so nice.

As we walked home together, my dad talked to me about the importance of keeping a commitment regardless. Not only did this teach me the importance of keeping my word, it also taught me the value of being on time. Ever since, being on time is almost like a badge of honor with me.

This was a great lesson, and one reason why I appreciate my dad. One time in a small group meeting, everybody in the room was asked to say who the most influential person in their life was. Even though I left home when I was 18, my dad was my most influential person, because he always talked to me in a reasonable manner. Not in anger, not in punishment. That really helped me relate to him, and I really appreciate the way he raised me.

I was really a naughty and active little boy, and I gave my mother a lot of trouble. Once I had done something particularly bad, and when my dad got home from work, my mom started complaining about it. Taking me into a bedroom, he closed the door and told me, "Start screaming." Then he started clapping his hands to make it sound like he was giving me a good spanking. I started screaming, and soon my mom was at the door. "Abraham! Stop!"

Another time when I was older, her constant complaining about me made him so mad he started throwing things. He broke all the dishes and everything in the house. Then he calmed down and took my mother out to buy everything new. But he never hit me in spite of it all.

ONE YEAR OF COLLEGE

In my first year of college in Beirut, Lebanon, I met this African-American girl—a very nice, sweet girl named Marilyn Hubbard. She was a student at the American University, and as a black girl, one of a kind in that country. Her father was the American Counsel in Pakistan. I invited her to come and spend the weekend with my sisters at my house in Tripoli, 50 miles away.

That Saturday night there was a dance at our country club. I didn't get to dance with her once! All my dad's friends wanted to show respect to my dad, and they all lined up to dance with her. I was so mad that I got shut out.

At one point that weekend my mom asked me to run errands for her. Marilyn, not understanding my mother's Arabic, thought she was yelling at me about something, when she was actually telling me what she wanted from the store.

There's no prejudice against black people over there, and I came to America without that prejudice in my heart. I didn't see Marilyn as anything but my friend. That lack of prejudice helped me to deal with the Black Panthers when I was at McDonald's in Kansas City after the assassination of Martin Luther King.

THE MOUNTAIN HEALER

During my one year of college (which I didn't
finish) in Beirut, Lebanon, we played pick-up
basketball. Once a tall American kid hit me
with his knee and whacked my right thigh. It
hurt, but I kept playing.

By that night, my thigh was so swollen I was
in excruciating pain. I went to the American
hospital in Beirut, probably the best medical
care available. I was there for two days. They
gave me medicine that didn't do any good. On
the third day, the thigh was still swollen, with
ugly shades of green, blue, red and black. My
dad came from Tripoli to Beirut to find out
what in the world was going on.

The doctor told him they couldn't do anything
more.

So my dad got me in his car, and we drove the
50 miles to Tripoli. He had heard of a guy in

the mountains, an old man, not a doctor, who could take care of these kinds of things. It took another hour and a half for us to get there.

This old villager looked at my leg, and he said, "I can help you, but what I'll do will hurt very much. When I'm done though, you're going to walk out of here."

First he prepared some hot oil from lamb fat. The sheep in the Middle East have a fatty tail. He heated some of that fat to melt it and started rubbing that hot oil on my leg.

"You can scream all you want, because it's gonna hurt."

With both hands he was pressing on my leg very forcefully. And I mean I was screaming my head off. This went on for a half an hour, him squeezing my leg and me screaming. More hot oil, more pressure. But afterwards he wiped his hands, and I was able to walk to my dad's car. They carried me in, but I walked out. I was just in the American hospital that morning, and now I was healed. The old man saved my leg.

That night, I drove my car back to Beirut and went to a dance!

CHURCH IN LEBANON

People are always asking me if I was a Muslim and converted to Christianity. That's not the case. My family were always Christians (as a matter of fact, my mom and dad's cousin was the Anglican Bishop of Jerusalem), and my parents used to take us to church. My dad would give us some change to put in the collection. I used to sit toward the back, and by the time that velvet bag with two wooden handles got to me, it was full of money. So I would put my hand in and shake the bag with my empty hand so it sounded like I put my money in. I never did, but it sounded like it! Then I used my money to buy ice cream and go to the movies.

I think it was at that time that God said, "I'm gonna get this guy!"

LIFE IN BAGHDAD

MY BUSINESS IN BAGHDAD

In 1958, I was in college in Beirut when the problems between Christians and Moslems in Lebanon escalated into civil war. This was the time President Eisenhower sent the Sixth Fleet into the Mediterranean to protect American interests in Lebanon. I would have been called up to fight, and my dad was worried about my safety. We had relatives in Iraq, and he thought I would be safe there with them until the war was over.

I arrived in Baghdad on July 7, 1958, to stay with my Aunt Frida and Uncle Najeeb and their four kids. The following week, on July 14, 1958, a revolution there resulted in the overthrow of King Faisal II. He and the entire royal family were killed, along with all the generals and colonels that were loyal to him.

Three days before the revolution, I had found a job at a company that distributed books and magazines. But now there was a new law in Iraq that no foreigner could work in an Iraqi company, so I had to leave my first job. The guy who owned that company said, "Listen, Nabil, I trust you. You've shown you're a good employee. Open a small shop, and I'll supply you with books and magazines for you to sell." So that's what I did, and I sold records and albums there, too. My shop was located near the embassies, and most of my customers were American, British, and French. I would eventually have about 200 subscribers to *Time*, *Newsweek* and the *Herald-Tribune*, which my 12-year-old cousin and I delivered if they passed censorship.

Then, a guy named Tommy Parker from Dallas told me about American hamburgers. He thought the Americans in Baghdad would love to have a hamburger. So I rented a Coca-Cola shack, bought ground meat and buns, and opened up in the evening after closing my shop.

Every night I sold everything I had.

I parked that shack at a very busy bus station, and people would line up. It was phenomenal. I would have to send my cousin out to the line to count off the people to match the number of hamburgers I had left. Then I'd have to say I could only serve that many more. Between my shop and the hamburger stand, I was a tycoon in Baghdad, making a lot of money.

ARRESTED IN BAGHDAD

Sue Folsom was the best customer at my
shop. She was about 40, and told me she was
secretary to the ambassador. We became good
friends, going out to eat or to listen to music
when we could.

One Monday morning, two well-dressed men
approached me at the shop and asked me to
go with them. "I'm sorry," I said, "I've got all
these magazines and papers to deliver." But
they gave me no choice. The men informed me
that I was under arrest. They took me to jail.
About noon I was taken to an interrogation
room where a captain and two sergeants sat
behind a desk. The captain said, "So you're the
American spy!"

What? I told him he was crazy. "You're not
only an American spy," he said, "you're a rude
American spy! Take him back to the cell until
he's ready to talk. We have 11 people to hang

on Saturday. He'll be the 12th."

I was shaken and terrified. My cousin Raja and I used to be spectators at the square as people would be hanged. And now I'm one of them?

In my pocket, I had the card of a friend of my father's, a colonel who was the head of the military academy in Iraq. He was neutral and not with the king or the revolution. I asked the prison guard to call the colonel for me after he was off duty. I gave him three dinars, which was all the money I had, and a lot of money for a soldier. When he left, I didn't know whether he would call the colonel or not.

At about 5:00 that afternoon I saw through the small window in my cell the army car with the colonel and his driver. I was brought into the interrogation room again, and the captain stood up with the sergeants to salute him. The colonel said to the captain, "What are you holding this boy for?"

The captain responded that I was spying for the Americans, British, and French. But the colonel starting telling him that I came from a good family, that my father worked for Iraq Petroleum Company and had built lots of housing in Iraq and that he himself had stayed with us in Lebanon for 10 days on his honeymoon. He then said he would take me into his custody. Grabbing me by the hand, we walked out.

In the car, the colonel looked at me sternly and asked what I was doing. "Nothing, Uncle," I told him. "These people are crazy and threatened to hang me!"

"Well, you must be doing something or they wouldn't have arrested you," he replied.

He had promised my father that he would look out for me, but under these circumstances, he couldn't. He told me to take Tuesday to put all my affairs in order, and he would drop by the shop around noon Wednesday to get me out of the country.

On Tuesday morning, Sue Folsom came to the shop and asked where I had been the day before. I told her the Iraqi Secret Service arrested me for being a spy, and she said, "They're crazy."

"That's what I told them!" I said.

"What are you going to do?"

"I don't know."

"Would you like to go to America?"

I knew nothing about America. I always placed second or third in my class— from the bottom. How could I go to America? But there she was on Wednesday morning with 10 different telegrams from 10 different universities. "Pick one," Sue said to me. I told her I enjoyed mountains and snow-skiing, so she said, "Go to Colorado State then. I'll make the arrangements. Go back to Lebanon, get your visa and get to America."

Years later, I was in Salina, Kansas, and was snowed in. I knew Salina was Sue's hometown. Scanning the phone book, I found the name Elnora Folsom.

"Ma'am, I know this is strange," I said on the phone, "But 21 years ago I knew a lady by the name of Sue Folsom from Salina. Would you know her whereabouts?"

"Who is this?"

"This is Nabil ... "

"Nabil!" It was her! She came to the motel where I was staying and picked me up in her big Lincoln. We cracked a couple beers at her house, and I said, "Remember how dumb those Iraqis were, picking on a kid like me, accusing me of being a spy?" "Oh no, they weren't dumb," Sue said. "I worked for the CIA."

I had been providing intelligence for Sue and others without knowing it, and thank God I didn't know it. I was actually passing information between Sue and officers from the British and French embassies. Sue would buy a book and then bring it back and tell me to sell it again. The next day Leo Coats from the British embassy would come in and ask me for a good book. I would recommend the book Sue had brought back and say I'd sell it to him for half price since it was used. He would always pay me the full price. The next week Leo would come in looking for a cha cha record. A few days later he would bring it back saying his daughter didn't like it. Then Maurice from the French embassy would come in and buy it for his fiancee.

Although my father wasn't a landowner and couldn't guarantee my return if I failed, the American embassy waived that requirement and facilitated my ability to get a student visa. As I was saying goodbye to my family at the port in Beirut, my father said something before I boarded the ship that was the complete opposite of what most parents would tell their kids.

"Son, don't come back."

COMING TO AMERICA

THE JOURNEY

From Beirut, my ship sailed across the Mediterranean Sea to Naples. There I boarded the ocean liner, The Julius Caesar, for New York. I planned to go from there to Boston to visit relatives before moving into the dorms at Colorado State.

But before I could get to Boston, I needed to find my luggage. When I disembarked, my suitcases weren't there. Over and over I looked through all the "H"s, but it wasn't there. Three hours and six hot dogs later, after all the luggage was claimed, there was mine, under the "N"s. The baggage handlers didn't know my first name from my last.

I spent a week with my relatives in Massachusetts, and then David Grahek, a friend of mine from the ship, had invited me to visit him in Lancaster, Pennsylvania. During my time there, Dave fixed me up with a blind date. "Why does she have to be blind?" I asked.

It's a family joke to this day.

I MEET PEGGY

I had settled into my dorm room at Colorado State and was beginning orientation. The first social activity was a freshman dance, so I went with my roommate and met this girl named Peggy Johnson. There were about five girls from Loveland, Colorado, standing there, and I looked at them, and Peggy's face just came right at me. Her face attracted me, so I went and asked her to dance, and she said yes.

She asked me what my name was, and I told her it was Bill. I didn't say Nabil in those days; Nabil did not mean much to Americans. Because of my accent, for two months she thought my name was Ben. She told me she was majoring in electrical engineering. That was fascinating to me, because nobody where I come from would have a woman going to engineering school. She's extremely smart and was a top scholar in the state of Colorado. She graduated from high school as a

Boettcher Scholar, which was the number one scholarship in the state of Colorado, and she was the homecoming queen in Loveland. I was impressed with her. She was impressed with the way I danced.

The next Saturday there was going to be another dance. For this one you had to bring a date, and I didn't know anybody except Peggy. My schedule during the week was to get up and go to an 8:00 meeting to show us freshmen around and talk about the university. She should be up, or so I thought. I called around 7:30 and woke her up. She was sleepy and groggy, but I said, "I was going to ask you to the dance next Saturday." She said yes.

So we got to know each other better, and from then on we just kept dating and going to functions together. I registered in some classes she did, and she registered in some classes I liked. We were together three months before I found out that she had a car. We had been walking everywhere, and it had begun to snow and be cold. Peggy told me she didn't want me to like her just for the car! We dated a whole year, and then the following September we were married. After that I figured if I'm man enough to get married, I should be man enough to support myself.

When I wrote my dad a letter about Peggy, I told him that same thing. That didn't work out so well. She had a good scholarship, and she lacked nothing. I had nothing. I had no money, so I began washing cars, cleaning dishes, and doing some odd jobs. Obviously I needed a real job.

I GET A JOB AT McDONALD'S

Obviously I needed a full-time job. McDonald's had a "Help Wanted" sign in the window, so I applied. I went back the next day, and the man told me he was still taking applications. On the second day, he said he was reviewing applications, and on the third day he was checking references. The days ticked away, and he wasn't hiring me. On the eighth day, I had a new plan.

"Sir," I said, "I see you're not going to hire me. But I'll make a deal with you: I'll work for you for two weeks for free. If you like me, hire me. If you don't, no hard feelings."

So the next morning I was in a uniform with an apron and a red crew hat, ready for work. Here I thought I was experienced, having sold hamburgers in Baghdad. Right off the bat, the man who hired me said, "Put on six patties."

I had no idea what that was. What's a patty?
Where do I put it?

"Walter!" he said. "Show him what a patty
is." Getting a little more exasperated, he said,
"Never mind, put six buns on."

I didn't know what a bun was either. Where I
come from, it's meat and bread.

But I figured it out, and I was shown how to
put mustard, ketchup, pickles and onion on
the burgers.

The owner wrapped five of the burgers and
pushed a tray toward me with one hamburger
left and said, "Cheese it."

I thought he said, "Eat it." Now, I was going
to show that I'm a man of endurance -- I don't
have to eat anything in the first five minutes of
work! I said, "No sir, I'm not hungry."

Now he was mad. "Cheese it!" I still didn't know what he was talking about. Where I come from, there's no such word as "cheese it." After the owner blew his top and said some other words I didn't understand, he told me to clean the bathrooms.

I had never cleaned a bathroom before, so needless to say I was apprehensive. Here's this kid coming to America to become an engineer, and he's cleaning bathrooms. But I saw a bucket, a chamois, and a sponge, and I cleaned that bathroom as best I could. He came back, thought the place looked really good, and said, "From now on, you can clean the bathrooms every day." After two weeks, I was happy to tell Peggy that I had earned a job at 80 cents an hour.

I WORK THE WINDOW

I used to work nights, and there were always four people working the night shift. Usually, me and another guy worked, and the other two played cards. At that time, there were two small windows at the counter for taking orders and people especially lined up on Sunday nights when the dorms at Colorado State didn't provide supper. The boss had specific instructions for me because of my accent: "You can cook fries and hamburgers, but whatever you do, stay away from the windows."

However, when the boss went on a vacation, the manager told me, "I want you to work the window."

"But you heard what he said. He'll fire me!"

"I'll tell him I told you," he replied. "If you don't work the window, *I'm* going to fire you!"

I worked out a system, pre-computer, where I added up the order in my head, told the customer the total and put together the food as that customer would get ready to pay. And I was very fast. If somebody would give me four hamburgers, two fries, two shakes and a Coke, I'd tell them how much it was, with tax. I was doing twice or three times the volume as the guy working the other window.

So guess who showed up unexpectedly on a busy Sunday night, fresh from his vacation? And who does he find working the window? The owner was furious, but the manager intervened and sought to calm him down. "Just watch him," he said.

I kept the routine, taking orders, adding them up in my head, sacking the order, making change. Every time I'd take an order and said how much it was, he'd run into his office and see if the totals were right. After a while, he took a reading at both registers to see the amount of the sales at each one. An hour later he took a reading at mine, and sure enough, I did three times the business as the other guy. Finding out how accurate and fast I was, he said, "If I see you working anything else but the window, I'll fire you!"

In three months, he gave me a raise and promoted me to an assistant manager.

HOW CAN YOU BE SO STRONG?

There was a kid who came into the McDonald's in Fort Collins, an ornery, belligerent high-schooler.

I said, "Sir, listen, what do you want? Let's just be calm about it."

"Okay, give me a bag of French fries."

Instead of taking it and paying for it, he took that bag of French fries and threw it at me, scattering fries all over the place. He was nasty, so I decided to be nasty back. I took the big ladle that was there and hit him right on the head with it. "Get outta here," I said.

Next thing I know, about a half-hour later or so, his older brother and half the football team showed up. "Are you the guy that hit my brother?"

"Is he the guy who ordered a bag of fries and threw it at me? If that's the guy, then I did hit him. There's no reason for me to hit your brother unless he did something wrong."

"Do you wanna fight?" they said.

"No, I'm running the restaurant. I don't need to fight."

The lobby was full of people. But again they said, "Do you wanna fight? Chicken...! Chicken...!"

"Okay, meet me at the side door." Then I told the only guy working with me, "Call the police."

I went out there and walked up to the kid, all 120 pounds of me, and popped him one time. He just dropped to the ground. With my dukes up I said, "Who's next?"

Nobody.

"Okay, you guys better pick up your buddy and get outta here."

The next day, all of them came back. "Hey, we're fighting another high school. You want to come with us? How can you be so skinny and be so strong?"

When I said no, they challenged me to an arm wrestling match with the biggest one, but he couldn't put my arm down, even using two arms. "How can you be so strong?"

GOING TO KANSAS CITY

My owner had a plan to expand and purchase more McDonald's franchises. He was able to make a deal to move to Kansas City where there would be an opportunity to do that. He offered me a managerial job promising that after five more years, he would give me 10 percent of the business if I would go with him to Kansas City.

Five years in, a few months before he was supposed to give me that 10 percent ownership, a man came up to me and said, "I've been watching you work. You're really good. Is that beat-up Volkswagen yours?"

"Yes, sir."

"I'll give you a brand new Chevrolet, and I'll pay you double what he's paying you, because I know he can't be paying you more than $1,000 a month."

"No, sir," I said. "Thank you, but I have a vision for where I'm going. I'm going to stay right here. Thank you for noticing me though."

By this time, the owner had two McDonald's in Kansas City. I was looking forward to being part owner of those two locations and of any others we would acquire as a partnership.

Soon after that job offer, the owner reneged on his promise to give me 10 percent. His plan had changed, and this time the plan was illegal. He told me, "You know, 10 percent of two McDonald's is a lot of money. Why don't you skim $2,000 a month, $1,000 from each restaurant? You give me one, you keep one. I won't tell on you, you won't tell on me."

I was crushed. Here I had told him I wouldn't do anything that wasn't legal when I started working for him, and I had never stolen from him.

"You're free not to give me what you promised," I said. "I'll stay with you for a short time until you replace me, but I'm not going to do anything dishonest."

Then he did quite a bit of groveling. "I'll give you 20 percent!" he insisted.

"Listen, you don't understand," I said. "Even if you gave me 90 percent and you kept the 10, I still wouldn't stay. I can't work for you anymore under any circumstances."

I knew I could find another job. I just needed to convince someone to hire me. A friend of mine happened to own a small plane, so I asked him to fly me to Chicago to meet with Fred Turner, who was the president of McDonald's. I would give him the first shot at me.

LIFE AS A
BUSINESS OWNER

GETTING MY OWN McDONALD'S

I had never met Fred Turner before and didn't have an appointment. The secretary said that he was really busy, but I said, "I can wait." It was an agonizing wait. I felt my future depended on this meeting.

After two or three hours, it was my turn to go into his office. I introduced myself and told Mr. Turner that I had worked for McDonald's for eight years and that I couldn't continue with the job that I held, but that I wished to stay with the company if it was possible. He asked me who I worked for. I told him the name, and he said, "You worked for *that* guy *that* long?"

"Sir," I said, "He taught me everything I know. I'm here because I'm good, not because he's bad." I told him nothing about how the man had reneged on his promises, and I told him nothing about the skimming.

It just so happened that a guy walked down the hall behind us. It was the Field Consultant for the Kansas City territory, a man who had worked closely with me. Mr. Turner called out, "Hey Jack! Come on in. What can you tell me about Nabil Haddad?"

"Mr. Turner," he said, "he's the best manager we have in the whole country."

With that endorsement, Mr. Turner picked up the phone immediately and called the vice president in charge of franchise sales, Ken Props. "I've got a young man I'd like you to talk to," he said to Ken.

I heard a bunch of complaining on the other end. "I've got 12 people waiting!"

"Mr. Turner, I'll wait," I said. By then it was getting dark in Chicago, and I waited another hour or so before Ken called me in.

"How much money have you got?" he asked.

"I don't have any," I said. "As a matter of fact, I'm $700 in the hole."

"Oh, you must know Fred Turner then."

"No, I just met him for the first time." Ken was incredulous. He got on the phone and said, "Hey Fred, this guy doesn't have any money!"

I could hear Mr. Turner barking at him. "You find it for him!"

Click!

What he found were four locations for sale that were cheap: Mobile, Alabama; Bakersfield, California; Columbus, Ohio; and one that was losing money in Kansas City, Kansas. Well, I lived 15 minutes away from that location. Without even thinking, without even checking out the others, I said, "I'll take Kansas City,

Kansas."

The owner of that franchise wanted $150,000, so I applied for a loan at Home State Bank. I told the bank's president, Cliff Nesserod, that I had no place to go but up, that I'd make money and pay him back. He said, "I'll let you know tomorrow." Also, I borrowed some money from my aunt and my sister.

The next day, the bank approved my loan, and within a week, I was a restaurant owner. The first year I took that store from losing $15,000 to making $49,000 a year.

THE BLACK PANTHERS

When Martin Luther King was killed, the Black Panthers demolished almost every single storefront in Kansas City, Kansas. But they would come to me at my restaurant at 9th and Minnesota and say, "How come you're still open?"

"As you can tell from my accent," I'd say to them, "I'm not from here. If you knock this place down, I have insurance to rebuild it. But that is not what I'm here to do. I'm here to serve the community. I don't care what your color is: black, white or in between. If you come, I call you 'sir,' I call you 'ma'am,' and I'll serve you with all my heart."

They didn't touch me or damage my store and even gave me a number to call in case I needed help.

And, the community liked me. Kids that the

city and the police couldn't control, I was able to deal with and I was able to hire. One guy came to the window to order, and he started in on "mother-this" and "mother-that." I said, "Excuse me, let me talk to you in the back."

"What do you want?"

"Just come in the back, and I'll talk to you," I said. "Now listen, if another person comes in and your mother and sister are standing at the window and he's calling them names like this and pushing them around, what would you want me to do?"

He was stunned. Nobody had ever talked to him like that.

I said, "Why can't you just come and work for me? I'll teach you something: manners, how to work, how to make money. I'll help you get your act together."

And he came to work. Everybody from the judge to the police chief to the mayor was astounded. How in the world did you get this guy to be so good?

The simple answer is, he had nobody to love him. And a lot of people right now just need somebody to love them, not reject them.

When employees were intentionally being bad seeds, that's a different story though. I was short one guy at lunch once, and we were always packed at lunch. One guy who knew I was shorthanded says to me, "If you don't give us a raise, I'm going to quit."

"Go ahead. Here's the door," I said without flinching.

"If you let me go too, you'll be two short."

"Damn right. That's not your problem. That's my problem." I showed him the door. But just as he left and the door was about to close, two guys came in saying "We just moved here from Arkansas. We used to work at a McDonald's there."

"I'll have you fill out an application later," I said. "But for now, get a shirt and apron on. You grab the grill, and you grab the fries."

They knew what they were doing, and with that the lunch rush was back to normal. Things like that have always happened to me.

HAPPY MEAL

Despite what Bob Bernstein would tell you,
I was the one who started the Happy Meal
when I was at McDonald's. In my location at
87th and Blue Ridge Boulevard, I did it as a
special promotion — a hamburger, french
fries, and a Coke, in a special bag. I called it
the Happy Meal after the popular TV show,
Happy Days. I also decorated my restaurant
with nostalgia items from the 1950s, and every
half an hour my guys would take a mop, play
"Rock Around the Clock" by Bill Haley and
His Comets, and mop the lobby and dance.
It was such a phenomenal promotion. We
jumped from an average of $700 a day to
$3,500 a day.

From there I took that promotion to all
my other restaurants. The president of
McDonald's came to see the Happy Meal, and
he was so impressed that they wanted it to go
nationwide. The ad agency for McDonald's,

Bernstein and Rein, took credit for starting it, but they didn't start it. They merely took it nationwide. The original idea for the Happy Meal was mine. And I have witnesses to back me up!

I had a lot of other promotional ideas like kite flying contests and Easter egg hunts, which we would have at Swope Park every year. Some of those events drew hundreds of kids.

THE CROWN PRINCE

One day I got a call from Victor Swyden, who was a city councilman of Lebanese descent. I knew him because I was working with him on a zoning question. "Hey, Nabil," he said. "The crown prince of Bahrain wants to meet you."

"Why?"

"He's fascinated with McDonald's. He's in Leavenworth at the War College learning to become a king."

Victor told me that one of his passions was playing golf. So I arranged a golf outing with Alex George, also of Lebanese descent, Victor, the crown prince of Bahrain, and myself. I had joined Meadowbrook Country Club, which was traditionally an all-Jewish club at that time, and I was the first non-Jewish member (or Arab member, for that matter).

When I called the club to make a tee time I told them I wanted three carts. "We understand two carts, but there are only four players. Who's the other cart for?"

"That's for the two bodyguards, because they're coming with the prince."

Meadowbrook was very gracious because they really gave us a lot of room. There was nobody in front of us, nobody behind us. The crown prince was very glad, and he played good golf. The only other thing he wanted was an automatic pistol. We were able to get one for him from the chief of police of Independence, Missouri, who was one of Alex George's cousins.

Hamad bin Isa Al Khalifa has now been the King of Bahrain for 16 years.

BEYOND McDONALD'S

McDonald's was fighting with my brother. Every time they wanted to bring a new McDonald's to Houston, he wanted it. "Get rid of your brother," they said to me, "and we'll give you 10 new McDonald's in the next year. We want you to stay."

Blood being thicker than water, I told them, "No. I'm done." It was at this time that my brother and I laid the groundwork for a new group of restaurants in Kansas City to be called Chutes.

From the time we started thinking about Chutes until it came into operation, it was exactly six months, which isn't easy. We wanted three drive thru lanes, one at the window next to the building, the second one farther out, and the third one farther than that, just as you would see at a bank. So what we did was contact a company in Denver that made pneumatic tubes like they use in banks. It was phenomenal, and people loved it. We served everything from hamburgers and hot dogs to chicken, submarine sandwiches, and pizzas.

Here's the problem, though. McDonald's bought our franchises for $5 million in restricted stock, which meant that we couldn't sell that stock for two years. When we were getting Chutes up and running, McDonald's stock was valued at approximately $62 a share. Everybody I talked to in brokerage firms said that it should increase to $102 and almost $110. So we figured we were safe. We borrowed money against the stock, and what happened was the exact opposite — the stock began to plummet. In less than a year, the stock was valued at $27 to $28 a share.

Two banks fought for my collateral, and that's what bankrupted me. We had to close everything down and sell everything. We had opened seven Chutes locations, and we had one more under construction that we couldn't even finish.

It wasn't that we didn't know what we were doing—the concept worked—it was the stock value of McDonald's that doomed Chutes. The headline on the business page of the Kansas City Star said, "Fast Rise, Fast Fall in Fast Food."

OUR SONS GO TO WORK

Now we were bankrupt. My two oldest
sons were 15 and 16, and Peggy and I had
no income. The boys got jobs delivering
mail for a courier service. They would
deliver mail before school and bring home a
couple hundred dollars a week for us to buy
groceries. They did a really good job helping
me when I was down. To reward them, I told
them I'd pay for their education as long as
they wanted to go to school. Abe went to art
school and David went to KU and majored in
business. I also said I'd buy David any car he
wanted, and typical of his low-key style, he
wanted a Volkswagen.

After a year or two of school, David changed
his major to Spanish. He came to me and said,
"Dad, in order for me to do well in Spanish, I
need to go to Spain for a summer."

So he went to Spain as an exchange student

and lived with a family in Barcelona. We didn't hear from him the first month. I was kind of worried about him. What happened to that kid?

But one night I got a phone call. "Hey Dad!"

"How are you? I haven't heard from you!"

"Oh Dad, Dom Perignon is $25 here! Send money!"

Abe went to the Kansas City Art Institute. Our daughter graduated with honors from the University of Kansas and then from Georgetown Law School where she was editor of the Criminal Law Review. Our youngest son became a luthier and worked for Gibson Guitars.

PAINTING MY HOUSE

We sold cars and Peggy's jewelry so we
could have some money, and we were really
struggling. Every once in a while I'd look in
the paper to see if there was a job I wanted
to apply for, but there wasn't. Who's going to
hire me anyway? I'm an entrepreneur who's
just lost a few million dollars. What company
would hire me so I could lose a few more
for them? And so I'd sit in my pajamas by
the window in our Fairway house and read,
devastated and withdrawn.

When I'd pray to the Lord, He'd say, "Paint
your house." It was all scraped up and the
Home Owners Association was complaining. I
didn't have the money to paint it though. I had
sold everything we owned. We were down to
nothing.

Finally a guy from church said to me, "What's
the Lord telling you?"

"He keeps telling me to paint my house. And I don't have any money to buy paint."

"I have an account with Benjamin Moore," he said.

I asked Peggy what color she wanted, she told me, and I went there and bought one gallon of paint on Frank's account. But we really needed 11 gallons. Peggy thought she was going to have a striped house.

And I hated painting. I can dig ditches, I can clean anything you want, but I absolutely detested painting. To make matters worse, it was so hot that summer that it would be over 100 degrees in the afternoons. I'd paint for five minutes and then cool off for half an hour. And this went on and on and on. Once again I said, "Lord, I can't believe you're doing this to me. It's hot as hell and you're making me paint my house."

He answered, "If you had painted it six months ago when I told you, it was cool then!"

The day I finished painting the house, I got a phone call from my younger brother, William, saying the company he was working for was going to be looking for people with my kind of experience. So I borrowed a suit from my dad – I had gained weight since quitting smoking – and applied for a job with that company.

I GO TO WORK FOR SAMBO'S

So I finally got a job supervising seven Sambo's Restaurants in seven different cities in the Midwest, from Effingham, Illinois, to Paducah, Kentucky. I would fly from Kansas City to St. Louis and then have a car at the airport so I could drive to all seven locations. They were all high-volume stores, but they were so separated that nobody was able to control them, and they were called "The Snake Pit" by the company management.

When I was assigned that territory, they told me to fire six of the seven managers, and to keep the one in Mount Vernon, Illinois who they claimed was the only good one. My boss asked me at our first meeting, "What are you going to do in sales in your stores next month?"

I projected a 5.5 percent profit, and he laughed so hard that he fell backwards.

I had my boss drop me off in Sikeston, Missouri, so that all seven managers could meet me. I went in there and sat at the conference table. In the first 10 minutes, all I heard from them was a barrage of complaints about everything the corporate headquarters was doing.

I finally got up from my chair and looked out the window at the parking lot and the surroundings. One of them said, "What are you looking at?"

"I just want to know if I'm in the right place," I said. "Listen, I can understand your hardship. Why don't you, all of you, leave your restaurant keys on this table, go to your restaurant and pick up whatever you have and just go home? I understand how bad you feel. I don't want you working for me or the company if you feel this bad."

One of the others said what they all were

thinking. "What are you going to do? You can't run seven stores by yourself."

"You know what?," I said, "That's not your problem. All I'm saying is I don't want you to be so unhappy that you don't want to work here. I totally agree with you: Nobody can do anything about it except you and me. If you don't want to, I'll understand. But they hired me to do something about it."

None of them left their keys there that day. All the guys they told me to fire, I didn't fire. But the one they told me not to fire is the one I fired, because I thought he was a rebellious hot-shot.

At the end of the first month, we ended up with 6.5 percent profit and freaked my boss out. We started making a profit like they'd never seen for the next several months. The vice president called me and said, "Nabil, I'd like you to come to Chicago. Leave everything and come right now."

I said I couldn't come immediately because I had a commitment on Sunday night. I was giving my testimony at a church in Mayfield, Kentucky. I said I'd see them as soon as I could on Monday. When I got to Chicago that Monday, the vice president asked his secretary to get him my file. She came back and told him the file was empty. There were no copies of correspondence between me and my managers. I told him I didn't need correspondence to prove I was working. My figures spoke for themselves.

He told me, "I have good news and bad news for you. The good news is we're going to promote you to territory manager. Now you have the territory of Kansas and Missouri. The bad news is that the office for that territory is in Kansas City, not St. Louis. So you have to move to Kansas City." I said, "Okay, I have two pieces of good news. The first bit of good news is that I get to be a territory manager instead of a district manager. The second good news for you is I live in Kansas City."

He was shocked. He said, "What? You mean to tell me you ran that district from Kansas City?"

Later they wanted to make me vice president, but this time, I turned the promotion down.

One of my most successful managers at Sambo's licked his fingers while he cooked. I shut his store down once even though it was open 24 hours because it was so filthy, and I issued him an ultimatum because he weighed more than 300 pounds.

"I don't want fat slobs working for me. I'm putting you on the scale every week."

Now this is obviously something you absolutely cannot do today. But he accepted, and he turned his store around. Within a few months he made a 21.5 percent profit and he was named Manager of the Month!

THE PLANE CRASH

Eventually, my business included several restaurants in other cities so I bought a small plane, a twin engine 421 Cessna. I would use the plane for business trips, but one time my pilot, my son David, and I flew down to Florida to play golf. Before we flew back, I noticed that the right engine was not pressurizing. You test all that before you take off, and I told Jim, the pilot, "That pressure on the right engine is down again."

Jim said, "Oh, once we get up in the air, it will be okay."

He insisted on going, so we did. Right as we were climbing, at 1,800 feet, the engine started sputtering worse, and it caught on fire. So we pushed the button to put the fire out, and Jim radioed the tower to tell them about the engine trouble. We turned around to land with the runway in sight, but the tower told him not to land on that runway but to go around to the main airport.

So here we are trying to land at stall speed, and I said, "Jim, listen, I'll pay the fine. These guys are not pilots. Land!"

I told David who was sitting in the back, "Put your head down. We're going to crash." We turned around on a dead engine, and we couldn't climb fast enough. Soon we started hitting street lights and the tops of trees.

The Lord spoke to me at that time very clearly: "Stay calm. You're going to be all right." We kept hitting bushes until a big tree stopped us, and we ended up crashing in an office park.

Both wings, with their fuel tanks dangling over the fuselage, blocked the pilot's door. Taking my briefcase, I followed David and scrambled for the passenger door. We were both unharmed. We helped Jim out of the pilot's seat and moved away from the plane.

An investigator with the FAA showed up and started asking us questions. "Who are you?"

So I gave him my name and number and other pertinent information.

But he kept asking, "Who are you? Who are you?"

I said, "Sir, I told you who I am."

He said, "Any crash like this with a 421 Cessna, whether it was in the trees or in the field, would've exploded." And he was shocked that it didn't.

The only one who got hurt in the plane was Jim, who broke his jaw. It was really a miracle to me, the fact that God spoke to me and said, "Stay calm. You're going to be all right."

Jim confirmed how calm I was, which was noticeable since I am usually fidgety.

The next morning I went early to the office because the plane crash was on the news. I wanted the office people to know I was okay. The first call I got was from Wayne Newton who said to me, "How's Evel Knievel?"

COMING TO
CHRIST

I HEAR FROM GOD

At one point I felt I had achieved all my
objectives—being a millionaire, power,
position, stocks—now what? When I was a
little kid, I used to curl up in bed every night,
depressed. I had no reason why. I had a nice
home with my dad and mom, I was fed well,
and I went to good schools and was on the
soccer team, which is a real honor in Lebanon.
Now, even with all of the success I had
achieved, combined with a wonderful wife and
four kids, the depression crept in again.

One night after Peggy and the kids had gone
to bed, I went down to the family room. I
really didn't want to watch TV — it was a
little after midnight. I just wanted to look at a
Bible to see what it is that Jesus has to say. All
I knew about the Bible was that Genesis was
at the beginning, Revelation at the end, and
the last part was the New Testament. We had
a big Bible at the house with a picture of Jesus

on the cover, and I flipped to the first page that had His words printed in red. Why is it that He died 2,000 years ago and people still talk about Him, and some even worship Him?

I didn't finish reading the first word in red when the Holy Spirit spoke to me. "I'm glad you asked that question."

And I suddenly understood that the Spirit was showing me that Jesus is the Son of God. Everywhere I looked, I could see the image of Jesus. There was a baseball game on TV, and He was right there on the mound. I could see Him in the trees and the clouds for days.

The next morning, I couldn't wait to tell Peggy. She was standing in the kitchen, and I said, "Honey, you're not going to believe what happened. Last night, God picked me out of six and a half billion people in the world and showed me that Jesus is His Son." Her answer to me was, "So?"

"What do you mean, 'So?' Don't you understand? There are six-and-a-half billion people on the face of the earth and God chose me to tell me that Jesus is His Son."

"Well, what are you going to do about it?"

I didn't realize that God reveals Himself to lots of people until she told me.

Every one of us has one or two or three people that, no matter how bizarre a thing you tell them, they believe you. So I called two friends, Todd and Denny, who both owned McDonald's. I told them what happened and the three of us went to a religious bookstore, parking my gold Rolls Royce in the back so nobody would see us, to buy Bibles that we could understand. We took them into my office, locked the door, and told my secretary, "No calls, please." We got together to read the Bible every day after that, and I mean it was phenomenal.

On July 7, 1977—7/7/77 —Peggy got two elders from the church to help me officially receive Jesus as my Lord and Savior.

After that, things in my life began to deteriorate. If I bought a stock, it would plummet. If I would buy silver, it would go down. Everything I did had the opposite result of what I intended. I didn't have my golden touch anymore. I got angry with God and said, "I can't believe this is happening to me."

He said, "I understand. Your power's gone, your stock is gone, your position is gone, your millions are gone. I'm going to take all these false gods away from you to show you who the true living God is. But I will restore you."

I used to run a mile in high school and would never sweat, but I tell you, I was sweating. And He did. He took everything. Everything. Within a few months I was bankrupt. But God did not renege on His promise to restore me.

Before the court had declared me officially bankrupt, I was a millionaire again and was able to repay all my creditors.

I LEARN ABOUT HEALING PRAYER

When I accepted Jesus as my Lord and Savior
in 1977, our church had a tour of Israel with
Derek Prince planned for the following spring.
We raised the money to go by selling our Rolls
Royce. On that trip, a group of 50 went from
Kansas City to New York, and from New York
to Germany en route to Israel. In Germany,
Derek spoke for 45 minutes and asked to pray
for people for healing. He said, "I want to start
with anybody who has been diagnosed with
one leg shorter than the other."

Three girls raised their hands, and they came
up front. Three chairs were brought for them.
Derek lifted the feet of each one in turn and
measured the length of their legs. He asked
them whether they wanted the short leg to
grow out or the long leg to shrink. The tall
girls wanted the long leg to be shorter, and the
short girl wanted her short leg to be longer.
Then he prayed that God would heal the

unevenness. I was sitting right in front, and I was watching to see what happened. When the prayer was finished, each pair of legs was miraculously the same length. Skeptical, I told Peggy, "Honey, that's a set-up."

Next, they brought up a little girl, two or three years old, who had never spoken. Derek put one hand on her mouth and one hand on her ear and said, "You dumb and deaf spirit, come out of her in the name of Jesus." She screamed, and it was the first time she made a sound. Still skeptical, I told Peggy again, "That's got to be a set-up."

Throughout the next hour, he prayed for people, and the miracles were incredible. I could not remain skeptical, could not continue to doubt what I was seeing.

From there, we flew to Austria, and from there to Tel Aviv. At the airport in Austria, I was collecting passports for all these 50 people that were on the trip, helping with the boarding process. I handed them to this lady behind the counter. She asked me, "Who is this group?"

I said, "See this guy over there?" And I pointed to Derek and told her about what he did in Germany.

"I have a leg shorter than the other. Would he pray for me?" I went to one of the leaders who was our missionary in Germany. "Hey, that girl has a leg shorter than the other. She asked me if Derek could pray for her."

When we went to Derek, he looked at us and said, "You guys go pray for her."

Now, I'm not about to do it, because I've never done that before. But Terry did as Derek had done, sat her in a chair, measured her legs against each other, and prayed for her. Sure enough, one leg shot out and became equal to the other. The baggage handler standing there dropped the bags and took off running. We never saw him again.

Now I knew for sure it wasn't a set-up. I wasn't skeptical anymore. There was no question in my mind that it was real.

TRAVELING WITH DEREK PRINCE

The summer of 1977 there was a big conference to be held at Arrowhead Stadium. Derek Prince was going to be one of the speakers. I offered him the use of my gold Rolls Royce while he was in Kansas City. But I didn't want to be the driver, so they got somebody from our church to drive him. Sure enough, that someone bashed the door, and Derek felt really bad about the damage. He wanted especially to meet the guy who owned the car, so that's how we met. I told him not to worry about it: "It's a piece of metal. It can be fixed."

He had heard about my conversion, but he asked me more about it and what happened. And when I told him, he felt like an Arab meeting Jesus was pretty unusual! So he invited me to go with him on a trip, and I did. Over an 18 year period, Derek and I went on many trips to numerous countries, and from then on, every time he came to Kansas City he stayed at our house, and we became friends.

I was not tagging along to help on these trips, even though I did. I would speak also, often in front of large crowds of 5,000 to 7,000 people. One time, in the morning when we were having breakfast in Africa, Derek said, "I'm going to speak today on righteousness. And Nabil, after I finish speaking, I want you to tell them how to apply it in their personal lives." In Africa, you sit in high chairs on a podium like you're a king. I was sitting there feeling a little petrified. What am I going to say after Derek Prince?

So I started speaking to these 6,000 African leaders, and for 35 minutes, I was like in a trance — I wasn't really aware of what I was saying. And when I finished, I walked by Derek and his wife, Ruth. She looked at me and said, "We never compliment speakers, but this is the best I've ever heard." And I sat next to my wife and I said, "Peggy, what did I talk about?"

Since then, Derek told me, "Don't rely on notes. Speak from your heart." So when I speak to groups of people, it's always unrehearsed.

I PRAY FOR A MAN IN JERUSALEM

When the tour group arrived in Jerusalem, we were waiting in the hotel lobby to be assigned our rooms when an Arab man approached me and said, "Who's this group?"

I said, "See this guy?" And I pointed to Derek again, telling him about the miracles in Germany and Austria.

This man said, "I have been going to the tomb of Jesus for 40 days and 40 nights asking God to heal me. God told me he was going to send somebody to heal me on the 40th day, and this is the 40th day. Will you please ask him if he'd pray for me?"

He unbuttoned his shirt, and his whole body was full of sores. Every inch of it was full of sores. "I'll ask him," I said.

I went to Derek and told him about the man.

He looked straight at me with these piercing eyes and said, "He's an Arab. You're an Arab. You pray for him."

This was the first time I had ever in my life prayed for anybody. I had two simple choices: either do it or don't do it. I said, "Okay, I'll do it."

I'd been watching what they do, so I sat this man on a chair. I put my right hand on his shoulder, and I prayed for him in Arabic that by the power of the Holy Spirit, by the blood of Jesus, this man would be healed in Jesus' name.

I began to hear his bones inside his body cracking and moving. When I said, "Amen," I opened my eyes, he opened his eyes, and sure enough, his skin was white as snow. There wasn't one sore on his body. He freaked out, and so did I. I couldn't believe it. He went around without a shirt in the whole lobby of that hotel showing everybody that God healed him. I was on fire for the Lord when that happened, and that was how my ministry started by praying for the sick and evangelizing. Miracle after miracle after miracle happened because of my faith and their faith.

THE DUCK DINNER

I went to church one Sunday when I was
broke, and I heard a guy behind me named
Jim Drake say that he was also looking for a
job. I assumed he was bankrupt just like me.
So we invited him and his wife to come to our
house for dinner. "We'll fix duck," I said, "and
I have a few bottles of wine from my good old
days."

I also invited a friend named Ted Stone and
his wife because they knew Jim and his wife.
We had $55 in the bank to work with, and
Peggy made a great duck with orange sauce.
But that afternoon Jim called. "Hey, we can't
come. A friend of mine from Columbia, who's
my partner with Cheese Villa, is coming in
today and will be staying with us."

I said, "Bring him with you."

Then Ted called and said, "Listen, we can't

come. I unexpectedly have a friend in town named Rick Stucy."

And I said, "Bring him with you!" We had a great time, and that night, after dinner, we prayed for John Humphreys, the man who came with Jim Drake, and he received Jesus as his Lord and Savior.

Stucy came to me and said he had a job for me running a restaurant in Lone Jack, Missouri, if I was interested. John Humphreys also offered Peggy a job running his Cheese Villa, a wine and cheese shop on the Plaza. I'm thinking, there are two guys here that weren't even originally invited. One of them got saved, and both of them are offering us jobs.

Peggy started at Cheese Villa, and I began to plan the restaurant in Lone Jack with Rick. We got it up and running, but Rick didn't last very long. He got fired from his job, and I got stuck in Lone Jack running the restaurant.

Not long after that, Rick came to me and talked to me about a job at Winstead's, a hamburger place that had been a Kansas City institution for decades. "My partner and I are going to buy Winstead's, and we want somebody to run it for a few months until we tear it down and build our own development," he said.

So they hired me at $36,000 a year, plus a third of the profit in excess of what they were making before, and sales began to soar. The restaurants were making about $270,000, but the first year I took over we made a $749,000 profit! Now Sailors & Stucy didn't want to tear down Winstead's. They wanted to expand it. And my son, David, is the one who helped expand the company.

It seems to me that my motives were always clean. To try to do what's right. Motive is important. If your motive is only money, or your motive is to get richer, it doesn't always work out so well. My motive was always to help. It was helping Michael Florsheim to take care of his buildings, it was helping Winstead's to run that place and run it right. And I ended up owning both the buildings and the restaurants.

I SPEAK CZECHOSLOVAKIAN

I had a manager at Sambo's from Czechoslovakia named Ludwig Burich, who asked me, "Why are you different than all my other supervisors?" I told him I'd see him after 5:00 when he finished working.

I took him to Maranatha Church in Cape Girardeau, Missouri, a church that I'd never been to before. We walked in, and to my dismay, there was no preaching, just a band playing that night. We sat toward the back, and they played some songs. After the service an elder and the minister came to us, and they hugged me and said, "How are you, brother?" But they shook Lu's hand.

Ludwig took me aside, and said within earshot of both of them, "How did they know you're a Christian and I'm not? They hugged you, and they didn't hug me."

They said, "Would you like to be like him? We'll pray for you."

He looked at me, and I said, "Ludwig, this is your opportunity."

So they prayed for him to receive Jesus as his Lord and Savior, and as they were praying for him in English, I prayed in tongues. As we got ready to leave, Ludwig looked at me with astonishment. He said, "How did you learn to speak Czechoslovakian?"

I said, "Ludwig, I don't know a single word in Czechoslovakian."

"Oh my God. God was speaking to me through you. Nobody not born there can pronounce things like you did."

"What was I saying?"

"You were saying 'I am the Lord, and I want

you to give your life to me,' in pure Czech."

That was such a miracle to see that God can reach you everywhere you are. And Ludwig was so fired up that he helped a lady with a bunch of kids fix her tires that evening.

Ludwig would later work for me at Winstead's. Once he called me at the office and said, "Nabil, Paul my cook flipped out. Every time I talk to him he says, 'I'm Jesus.' So I locked him in the office."

I was 15 minutes away, and when I got there I opened the office door and said, "Hi Paul."

But he said, "No, I'm not Paul. I'm Jesus!"

"Let's go, Paul."

"I'm Jesus!"

"Okay, let's go," I said again.

We got into Lu's car and went to Paul's apartment five minutes away. You had to walk down some steps to his door, so Ludwig and I went first, but Paul stood there at the top of the stairs. He had dyed his hair black, and he wore a black shirt, black pants and black shoes. When I looked at him, his face looked like what I would imagine Satan would look like.

I said, "Come on down, Paul."

And he said, "I'm not Paul, I'm Jesus."

I said again, "Come on down."

Then I began to pray for him and said, "I bind you, Satan, in the name of Jesus. Leave Paul alone." He then tumbled down the steps and foamed at the mouth. When he got up, his face had changed. He looked at me and said, "This thing that came out was in me all my life." After that, he was all right.

THE BROTHERS FROM AFGHANISTAN

My youngest son, Kareem, would travel
with me when he was 4 or 5 and I worked for
Sambo's, and he'd pray for people. Mahesh
Chavda had laid hands on him one day and
prayed for him to receive the healing ministry.
I used to go and talk to my managers and one
of them said, "The other district managers
wanted me to fix them up with the best-
looking waitress. You come in here and want
to help me succeed." Every week I'd go to my
district and I'd help them, and once in a while,
Kareem would go with me.

The manager in Marion, Illinois, was a Muslim
from Afghanistan, a son of the last prime
minister. He asked the same question: "Why
are you so different?"

As I had with Ludwig Burich I asked him,
"What time do you get off work?"

"At five."

"I'll see you then." I believed that I should not steal time from our employer for evangelism. Honesty is an important witness.

When we met after his shift, I told him, "You believe in Mohammed, I believe in Jesus. I don't want to tell you who to believe in. Here's what I want you to do. Go home, turn your lights off, close the windows, shut the door, get down on your knees and say, 'God, I believe in you. Who do you want me to follow? Jesus or Mohammed?'"

By midnight, I was in Paducah, Kentucky, and he called to tell me what happened. He said, "I did what you told me, and I heard my mother's voice outside the window. My mother is in Afghanistan. She said, 'I never lied to you, son. The only way to the Father God is through His Son, Jesus.' What do I do now?"

I said, "I'll come tomorrow and talk to you."

The next morning, I prayed for him to receive Jesus as his Lord and Savior. "Your mother didn't lie to you. She told you the truth."

Two days later I was in Paducah again. He had told his older brother, who lived in Indianapolis, what happened. When his brother said he couldn't believe it, he told him, "You just come and meet this guy," They came right away so his brother could confront me.

That week I had Kareem with me, so we talked to him about what happened to his brother. "You could have the same thing," I said. "Just let us pray for you if you want to and then you can decide."

So I had Kareem lay hands on him and pray for him that Jesus would come into his heart and be his Lord and Savior. And let me tell you something. His expression was dark when he came in, but his face instantly became lighter. I said, "Listen, go look at yourself in the mirror. What happened to you?"

"I felt like something dark left my entire body," he replied. He went and looked at himself and said, "Not only do I look different, I feel different." And he became a believer along with his brother.

PRAYING FOR PHYLLIS

A woman named Phyllis was in the fellowship group from church that I led. One night, we were going around and praying for each person, praying for deliverance and any number of things. When it came to Phyllis, it was difficult. She stood up, and I stood up right in front of her to pray for her. It was obvious to me that the spirit of fear was in her. When I spoke to her and asked for the demon to come out of her, she spoke in a voice that we had never heard before — a man's voice.

The voice said, "I've been here a long, long time, and I'm not coming out!"

So I told her, "Phyllis, you have authority over that demon. You need to help. By the blood of Jesus, by the power of the Holy Spirit, I command you to come out of Phyllis in Jesus' name."

Phyllis couldn't say anything for a while. Finally she said, "I don't want you in me. I want you out!"

"You heard her," I said. "She doesn't want you in her. She has authority over you, and I have authority over you. In the name of Jesus, come out of her!"

And I mean, it dumped her, and she collapsed, and it came out of her.

IN CURAÇAO WITH MAHESH

I was in Curaçao with Mahesh Chavda, the evangelist and miracle worker, and his wife, Bonnie. As Mahesh was praying for the people, there was a lady on the opposite side of the room who was screaming. She looked and sounded absolutely atrocious. Her face was grey, she was shivering and cold, and all these leaders in the church in Curaçao couldn't help her. Mahesh said to me, "Go see what you can do."

I approached her, and she was overwhelmingly cold. I said, "Okay, Lord, what is that?" He said, "Bind the spirit of death."

I said, "Spirit of death, I bind you over that woman in the name of Jesus." The minute I said that, she stopped shivering and flopped down.

That same meeting, Mahesh, Bonnie, Peggy,

and I were standing at a podium in front of rows and rows of people. There were about 600 people who all wanted to come and be prayed for. The first 20 people or so came and were prayed for, but nothing happened. Zero.

I said, "Okay, God, this is embarrassing. What is going on? Why is it that nothing is happening?"

The Lord spoke to me and said, "You see all these people? They have the blue eye necklaces, they have charms of gold, they have all these satanic and demonic protections that they believe in. Until they renounce all that, they're not going to get healed or delivered."

So I said, "Mahesh, stop for a minute." And I told Mahesh what I had heard. He told the crowd, "Until you renounce this evil thing and not rely on that but rely on the Lord to deliver you and heal you, expect nothing to happen. So if you have all that stuff, I want you to bring it to the stage right here." And we had a huge pile of gold.

Mahesh told them, "Go ahead and sell this. I don't want you to rely on it because it's not going to help." Then he said, "Now, since you're obedient to the Lord, and you did what He said, you don't have to come here.

The Lord's going to heal you all at one time." So with a flick of his hand, every single one of them fell backwards, slain in the Spirit. The word from the Lord is the most important thing, and obeying the Lord is the most important thing.

IN ENGLAND WITH DEREK

We were in England with Derek Prince one
time when he was speaking at a conference
of about 3,000 people. Proper Britishers, they
were all nicely dressed. A young evangelist
was seated there with the leadership team,
a good-looking young man in his twenties.
We noticed a lady there dressed in white who
seemed to be fixated on him. I told Peggy, "See
this lady? Watch out when Derek talks about
lust."

Sure enough, when he came to lust, this lady
jumped up, grabbed this young evangelist by
his tie, knocked him down, and jumped on top
of him. Several men tried to separate them,
but they couldn't. I got up from my chair,
stood over them, and said, "You demon of lust,
I bind you in the name of Jesus." She just fell
backwards off of him. The leadership took her
away for counseling. The young evangelist got
up, straightened himself out and nonchalantly

said to me in his proper British accent, "Sure wasn't a good day to wear a tie."

That guy later came to my office in Kansas City and told that story word-for-word!

MY DAD COMES BACK TO LIFE

Unfortunately, my dad was a stroke patient for the last several years of his life. One day Peggy and I were at my parents' house visiting, and my father was sitting in a chair in the kitchen. Suddenly he started making these snorting noises with his breathing, and then his head slumped, and he quit breathing altogether. What to do? We didn't want to leave his body sitting in the kitchen.

He weighed about 200 pounds, so I dragged his body to their bedroom and laid him on the bed. Meanwhile, my mother wailed and changed into black clothes and put on dark makeup.

Peggy called for an ambulance. While we were waiting for them to arrive, we were praying to God in tongues and asking Him to receive his spirit. Suddenly my dad raised himself, sat up and looked at me.

I opened the door and called to my mother to tell her that my dad was alive. She didn't want to hear it, thinking I was trying to tell her he was alive in heaven with Jesus. She started howling again. But I said, "Mom, come and see," and when she came into the room, she was shocked. I told her, "The next time he dies, you've already made one scene, so you don't have to do it again!" The ambulance then came and took my dad to the hospital.

My dad lived four years after that incident, every year with a different setback. He'd go to the hospital, I'd pray for him, he'd get a little better and go home. But the last stroke he had put him in a coma.

The hospital called us three or four times to say my dad was dying. Each time the hospital called, we would go to tell him goodbye, but he didn't die. So finally, Peggy and I were there along with my sister-in-law and sisters, and I asked them to leave the room so it was just my dad and me.

I said, "Dad, I don't know if you can hear me, and I know you can't speak. But I hope you can hear me. I know you're hanging on to something. I don't know what it is. But if you're worried about my mother or my sister, I'll take care of them. I want you to rest in peace and not be worried about anything."

Peggy and I left, and my mother and sisters went back into the room. We had hardly left the Menorah Medical Center parking lot before my mother called me: "You're not going to believe it."

I said, "What?"

"After you left, I went into the room and your father opened his eyes wide open and winked at me. He looked like an angel. He looked so beautiful, winked at me, and died." More than anything, what I can take from that is that it shows you what it's going to be like in heaven.

MY MOTHER'S FUNERAL

Some people take death differently than others. When my mother died, my cousin, who did not know her very well but knew her some when he was a little kid, came from Canada for the funeral. As he and I were walking toward the casket for him to pay his respects, he was just bawling. So I put my arm around him and said, "Hey, it's okay." The funeral director came to me and rebuked me for being hard on him. "Listen, be nice to him," he said. "It's his mother."

"No sir, she's my mother. He is my cousin!" And even though she was my mother, it didn't affect me the same way. I have faith that I will see her in heaven.

CATERING FOR THE STARS

CATERING FOR THE STONES

When I didn't have a job after Sambo's, Peggy and I started a catering business. Peggy's a good cook, and I'm a good talker. The first catering job we did was at the church for a wedding. Pretty soon, we were in the catering business for the stars.

We were in Cedar Falls, Iowa, to do one night for the Rolling Stones during their 1981 American tour. They heard that there was an ice storm predicted, and they thought they could pull a trick by telling the promoter that they wanted a clambake. We pulled into the stadium to set up and were met by the promoter with the news that now they wanted a clambake.

I said, "Sure, we can do that" and rolled up the window.

Peggy looked at me like I was crazy. "Do you

know what a clambake is?"

"No, but we'll figure it out." I called the only fish company in the phone book.

"Hey, I'm looking for fresh lobsters, fresh clams, and mussels – everything for a clambake."

"We don't have any of that. The only thing we have is frozen rock lobster tails."

"No, you don't understand. This is for *Mick Jagger*. Where do you buy your fish from?"

"Des Moines."

"All right. Where do they buy it from?"

"Boston."

"Okay, get on the phone, and call all these people and tell them what I want, and ship it by air."

"You don't know how much that's going to cost!"

"It doesn't matter."

"Okay, I'm going to do it for you if you do something for me."

"What's that?"

"We've been trying to get four tickets for the concert, and we can't get any!"

"No problem. If you get me the stuff, I'll get you the tickets." Again Peggy looked at me like I was crazy.

The seafood arrived in time, and I was able to get him four tickets. So Peggy's fixing lobster, and oysters and corn are getting shucked, and we had a long table set up in the hallway of the men's locker room. While the snow was blowing outside in northern Iowa, I had the place set up with birds chirping in all four corners, indoor/outdoor carpeting, groups of outdoor furniture, and hula dancers from the university. As the Stones walked in, they looked around and they were duly amazed! Mick Jagger said, "Who did this? I want to meet him!"

So I told him my name, and Mick said, "Listen, you know I can't eat before the show. But I want two of this, five of this, and six of this. I want this on my airplane when we leave!"

When it was time to be paid, I charged them $14,000 for the clambake, and Bill Graham, their famous promoter, balked. "That's too much!" he said.

But Mick just glared at him and said, "Pay the man."

When the Stones were talked into playing in Kansas City, Mick said, not knowing we were from Kansas City, "Here's what I'll do: You hire this guy to cater, and we'll do two shows in Kansas City."

So they played at Kemper Arena in Kansas City for two nights. The news program PM Magazine did a feature on the Rolling Stones coming to Kansas City, and I was on the same show talking about the catering. The next day Mick was coming down the hall and looked at me and said, "I saw you on TV last night."

I said, "What do you want me to say, Mick? That I'm impressed that we were on the same show together?"

He said, "No, they gave you more time than they gave me!"

Mick brought his family from England to Kansas City because we were catering for him, and they loved it. His security kept following me and my son around, but he looked at them and said, "Listen, I know this guy. He can come and go any time he wants without someone following him around."

After the two days of shows here, Mick gave me a souvenir program and signed it. Bill Graham's secretary couldn't believe it. She had been trying to get one from him for the whole tour and he wouldn't give her one, let alone sign it. Chris Fritz, the promoter, offered me $2,000 for it, but my son, Abe, didn't want me to sell it.

CATERING FOR JOURNEY

Journey happened to hire us to do their shows in Kansas City, Wichita, and Omaha, and that was probably the hardest job we ever did. But it was a fun job.

They had a tour manager who was the most obnoxious person. One time Peggy was setting up the line for the buffet, and he came to complain to me about the food. He always thought we charged too much, and he put his finger in the food and started complaining about how it wasn't hot enough. Peggy was infuriated.

The lead singer, Steve Perry, and the rest of the band had me come into the dressing room after the show and drink Dom Perignon with them. The promoter said, "Hey, get me in!"

I told him I'd ask Steve.

"Hey, Steve, the promoter wants to have a glass of champagne with you."

Steve said, "Screw him, we already made him a lot of money! We don't have to be nice to him. But you did a really good job for us. We want you here!"

CATERING FOR VAN HALEN

Here's a band who was really tough to work for, and I had heard that ahead of time — Van Halen.

They had just come from a town where they had food so bad, David Lee Roth took it and threw it on the wall. But we really took good care of them, and they loved what we served them.

The promoter had us take Diamond Dave to Plaza III, but he also wanted an Italian appetizer, so we got an Italian appetizer from Figlio and made him a fantastic meal.

We can confirm one of Van Halen's demands. It really is true that one of the things they specify in their food contract is to take the brown ones out of the M&Ms!

CATERING FOR ARLO GUTHRIE

Of all the people we catered for, Arlo Guthrie had the most perceptive palate of anyone. When he would come to Kansas City he'd play at a smaller venue, usually at the Uptown Theater. He always asked for Chinese food, so the first time Peggy cooked for him, she made plum sauce for the crab rangoon. The next time he came, he ordered the same menu, and Peggy made the plum sauce. But for some reason she used a different brand of plum jam to make it with, and he knew it.

"Why is the plum sauce different than it was the last time?" he asked.

He nevertheless enjoyed it, showing how these musicians probably don't get good food very often.

CATERING FOR OTHER STARS

It was just automatic after a while that we would cater for all the big musical acts even though we were expensive compared to everybody else. When they asked for beef, we got them Plaza III steaks. We rolled in with china and silverware, and we had a portable kitchen and a propane stove. We pulled out all the stops for everybody, not just the Rolling Stones.

We did Barry Manilow's shows several times. He always requested linguine with clam sauce, and Peggy had never made that dish. So she made it for him that first night, and the crew got whatever they had on the concert rider. Barry came out and wanted to know who made that linguine with clam sauce because it was so good!

For another one of their shows, they asked us to do Middle Eastern food. Now these guys on the crew do all the hard work at these concerts making sure the stage and the instruments are right. They're always on a bus, always getting to the next town, and nobody really appreciates them. So when we made Middle Eastern food for Barry's roadies, I hired a belly dancer to come and entertain them. They loved it!

Here Manilow is sitting in his private dressing room, and he's hearing his roadies having such a great time, and he has to open the door. "What is going on?" he asked.

Another time, they asked for Italian food. So Peggy made an Italian menu, we had checkered tablecloths and invited a violin player and accordion player to play Italian songs for them!

LIFE WITH FRIENDS

FRIENDS: OS GUINNESS

We met Os Guinness through Christ Community Church when he was here to speak. It got to be a tradition that we would take the pastors and their wives and the speakers to our restaurant, Plaza III, for dinner while they were in Kansas City. We also often would offer hospitality for the people coming, and we had our limousine meet their flight. (The only one who would politely decline was Dallas Willard.)

Os would call us when he was coming to town for other things, and he would come and stay with us. One time he was invited by a group to come and make some videos, and this group was using a venue at the International House of Prayer in Kansas City. Everybody assumed that all the students at the IHOP Bible College would be the audience. We got out there, and we were going to listen to him talk and be part of the audience. But, unbeknownst to the group doing the videos, IHOP had declared a fast somehow, and the students were all unavailable to come and be a part of the audience. So here's Os recording this video and preaching to about four or five people, Peggy and me included.

Another time, he was invited to speak at KU and stayed with us for a few days. During the time he was here, we were giving a party at our place that involved the Chiefs. We had donated a luau and pig roast party for an auction and some of the Chiefs players were part of the package. Os joined right in, mingling with players like Tamba Hali, who was a rookie that year, and watching the hula dancers try to teach these big guys how to dance.

Os is one of our all-time favorite people who's also a really good sport. We own a restaurant in the country called Timber Creek that has a weekly karaoke contest. We set this up once to have Peggy and Os among the judges in the finals. It was the first time he'd ever even seen karaoke, and he picked the winner!

FRIENDS: CANON ANDREW WHITE

Andrew White, the "Vicar of Baghdad," is a phenomenal guy who works in Iraq under really tough circumstances. One time, all of his five elders coming back from Jordan disappeared, and he never saw them again. Another time he was speaking at our church, and in the first two minutes, his assistant came and interrupted him and told him his church, St. George's Church in Baghdad, had just been bombed. Someone went to an office and turned on CNN, and sure enough, they were mentioning it on TV.

Most of his church is women and children because of the large number of men killed in the fighting. Andrew set up an infirmary there with doctors and dentists to provide free health care. He also provides food for many families in the church. There are many people in our congregation who are still really connected with him.

When Andrew would come to our house for a few days, he would have seven or eight telephones that would work in every part of the world. He would negotiate hostage situations in all those Middle Eastern countries. And when the Palestinians and Israelis were asking for any mediation, his name would always come up on top. He was very instrumental in the Iraqi cease fire, and everybody in the Middle East respects him. The current Archbishop of Canterbury, Justin Welby, used to work for him when Andrew was at Canterbury Cathedral.

Yassir Arafat called his house once to wish his younger son a happy birthday, and his son said, "Tell him I'm busy!" But he did invite him to his birthday party. Arafat sent him a gift but was unable to attend. The older son wants to become prime minister of England, and I wouldn't be surprised if he does.

Andrew has multiple sclerosis, and he and a

doctor in Iraq developed a treatment for MS that is based on the patient's own stem cells. They somehow separate the stem cells out of the patient's blood and then inject them into a spinal area. Although it's not yet approved in America, it's radically improved his condition.

FRIENDS: DICK VERMEIL

Dick and Carol Vermeil had very negative feelings about Christianity when we first met them. Because some of the Christian football players and their wives may have pushed it too hard, Carol was especially vocal in her resistance to Christianity. But we got to be really good friends with them.

We had a suite at Arrowhead Stadium at that time, and I would get field passes and take some of our guests down on the field before the game. I started greeting Coach Vermeil, and we would go out to the middle of the field, and I would pray for him.

One time we were at Plaza III with Ravi Zacharias and a group that included our pastors. Dick came in and asked for me and was brought to our table. It happened that the Chiefs were playing Atlanta that week, — and Ravi lives in Atlanta. So Dick was talking about how hard it was going to be for the Chiefs to play Atlanta. He said, "We really need to be prayed for this week."

Peggy said, "Oh, good! Sit right down here. We'll pray for you!"

So all of these pastors and Ravi prayed for him. Sure enough, the Chiefs crushed the Falcons, and Ravi has never let us forget it.

Dick and Carol became very good friends and have stayed with us in our home many times. Dick usually calls me every Sunday, especially during football season, to discuss the games.

BEING A FRIEND

One of Dick Vermeil's good friends from St. Louis is Don Bryant, the founder of Bryant Family Vineyard in Napa Valley. Every time Don came to Chiefs games, my driver would pick him up at the Downtown Airport and bring him to the games.

I got a call from him around 8:00 one Sunday night after he had been at the game. "Nabil, I'm going to Europe tomorrow. I can't find my phone anywhere. Would I have dropped it in your limo?"

"I'll go look."

Sure enough, there was his phone in the back on the floor. I called him right away and said, "I found your phone. What time are you leaving in the morning?"

"Great. Seven o'clock."

"Here's what I'll do: I'll get my driver, and since it's only 8:00, he'll head out now and be in St. Louis by midnight."

"You'll do that?"

"Absolutely." So my driver went to Don's house and took his phone to him.

Several months later, we saw him in California at a meeting of a group that we were both involved with, and we happened to be seated at the same table. There were about 50 people in that room, and he got up and told this story with tears in his eyes. "This guy here sent his driver with my phone from Kansas City to St. Louis so I could take it with me!"

His wine is very, very restricted. As famous as Plaza III is, they don't get more than two bottles each year. But I'm on his list every year for a dozen or two bottles of Bryant Family wine.

FRIENDS: CARL PETERSON

One night I was at my restaurant, Fedora on the Plaza. Chiefs general manager Carl Peterson and his friend, Lori, came in for dinner. At that time there was a lot of criticism about him and his handling of certain issues. He came by to say hello and we talked about the Chiefs. We ended up having dinner together and really enjoyed the time. That was the beginning of a tradition of dinners together when he's in Kansas City. Now retired from the Chiefs and living in New York, he is still in town fairly often.

In the years that Peggy had the horse business, we were always trying to market horses and figure out how to get people like the Chiefs to get involved. So one time, Peggy's trainer had this idea of sending a letter to Arrowhead addressed to the "Unappreciated Offensive Line," inviting them out for a day of hunting and shooting and fishing. And it actually got to the right person.

Dave Szott was one of the great offensive linemen the Chiefs had at the time, and he called Peggy to ask if this invitation was for real. He organized a day to bring all the linemen out, and they had a great time and a steak dinner. Carl then heard about it, and part of how we got to know him better was because of the success of that day at the farm for the offensive line.

Joe Montana heard about the offensive line coming to hunt at the farm and bought each of them a good hunting gun as a thank you for their work protecting him that season. Then Marcus Allen wanted to come to the farm. I missed him several times that he came out. He called and asked me why I was avoiding him. I said, "Marcus, you have a lot of people around you all the time. I'm just giving you a little peace."

FRIENDS: MICHAEL FLORSHEIM

I met Michael Florsheim in an unfinished
office building overlooking the Plaza that was
owned by my partners, Richard Sailors and
Rick Stucy. They were having a party during
the annual Thanksgiving Plaza Lighting
Ceremony and had invited everybody involved
with their new project to see the lights come
on. Michael was in the petroleum and iron ore
business and was one of the invited guests.
Even though he was at one end of the room
with them and I was at the other end of the
room, somehow our eyes met.

Michael asked Rick, "Who's that guy over
there?"

"A partner in the restaurant division. Why?"

"I just want to meet him." So they walked all
the way across the room, and Rick introduced
us. Just like that he looked at me and said,

"Next time I come to Kansas City, I'm going to have dinner with you."

Sure enough, we arranged to have dinner when he was back in town, and an Orthodox Jew from Switzerland and a Palestinian Arab became very good friends.

Even though he was Orthodox and technically shouldn't have stayed in a Gentile's home, he stayed with us whenever he'd come to Kansas City. He had a son, Alex, who loved riding horses at the farm. This kid only rode in limousines and Rolls Royces in Zurich, but he came to the farm and was nuts about horses!

Once when they had been there for a week, Michael said to Alex, "Come on, we need to go to New York and have a memorial service for your grandfather." But he wouldn't go! So Michael looked at me and said, "Can you help us have a memorial service for my father here in Kansas City?" So Sherman Dreiseszun,

Frank Morgan, and I arranged it for him.

Michael would call me often, and I'd travel
with him to Israel. The first time Peggy and
I were in Israel, it was a security nightmare
because they couldn't understand why I'd be a
person who loves the Jewish people. Michael,
his mother, and his grandmother were all
Holocaust survivors. When he heard how we
were treated by the security that first time,
he said, "Next time you go to Israel, you come
with me."

We went with him in first class, and nobody
ever got off the airplane before us! When we
got off, the head of security was there, and
they had our bags there, and we walked right
by the customs lines. That Tuesday night,
they had a reception for Peggy and me and
a garden party with a band and about 125
people, including the cabinet and professors
from universities. They had me sitting right
next to Shimon Peres.

So he and I talked about the war between the Arabs and the Jews. Peres said — and this was many years ago — "In a couple of years we'll have peace."

But I said, "We'll never have peace until the Prince of Peace comes."

Then on Saturday night, the night before we were leaving, they had another garden party for us. Michael just wanted to show us that Israel wasn't doing the right thing by picking on people that love the Jewish nation, love the Jewish people, and love America.

Michael was an extremely generous man. Don't look at anything that he could end up buying for you, because if we were walking down the Plaza and Peggy would say, "That's a nice dress," the next thing you know it would be in our house.

When he died in his swimming pool,

apparently of a heart attack, his wife called me and asked me to take care of all of his affairs in Kansas City, which were many. I worked for months on it. He also owned many buildings in Manhattan, and it seemed like he had something to do with everything on Manhattan Island, so from Kansas City I would negotiate with the banks and make sure things were handled properly.

When I got everything done, his wife called me from Zurich and said, "You're the only person Michael spoke about who was honorable." She also said she was giving me those two buildings on the Plaza, the very buildings my partners used to own and where I met Michael in the first place on that Thanksgiving weekend. We would eventually sell them for a $2 million profit.

FRIENDS: GEORGE BRETT

When I owned the restaurants, Fedora and
Plaza III, I got to know George Brett when he
would often come in for a few drinks. The first
time we sat down for any length of time was
on a night the Royals got rained out. He called
me, and we met at Fedora and had dinner. I
said, "It's really funny how normally when
they have a rainout you go out with the guys
and drink. This time, you wanted to talk to
me." And that's when I reached out to him and
told him about my relationship with God. We
became good friends. We'd talk, and he'd like
my wisdom.

When we had a dinner once at Plaza III,
George's mother, who was a Christian, sat next
to me and was concerned about him. I told
her I prayed for him every day, and promised
I would keep talking to him. George later
gave me a big autographed picture of himself
that said, "You're the best and wisest friend

anybody could have."

George would visit the farm once every two or
three weeks, sometimes once a month. When
we had horses, he also fished and brought
his kids out to the farm to fish. One time he
brought Rush Limbaugh to the farm. This
was when Rush was always wearing suits and
flashy ties, and he was afraid we were going
to throw him in a pond. Rush is really funny,
and it was like that all day with him. He said
he had never caught fish, so we gave him a rod
and reel and he did catch a lot of fish.

He was on the air the next day and said that he
had been at my farm. My nephew from Florida
called and said, "I just heard Rush Limbaugh
say he was at your farm!"

When we went to Cooperstown with George to
see him inducted into the Hall of Fame, Rush
was there too. Peggy and I both said, "He'll
never remember who we are." He was on the

other end of the room and when he walked all the way to us, I was shocked. He said, "Hi Nabil! Hi Peggy!"

The only time I ever had a hole-in-one was when I was playing golf with George Brett at a tournament in Lawrence. I didn't see it as well as he did, but man, he pounced on me. "Hole in one! Hole in one! He's never had one!"

I still have the golf ball I used with George's autograph on it as a souvenir.

Somewhere around that time, across the street from Fedora, there was a grand opening of the new FAO Schwarz store. They brought in the Duchess of York, who had a new children's book she was promoting for the opening. Our company was hired to do the catering for the event. They were all kind of nervous because they wanted a celebrity to be there to meet Fergie when she came. They couldn't come up with anybody, so they called me and said,

"What are we going to do?"

I said, "The only Royal I know is George Brett."

So George came into the store with his oldest son, Jackson, who was just a toddler, and he was there with me to greet the Duchess when she arrived.

Next thing you know, Fergie asks for water, and everybody's so concerned about her water and whether she's wants still water or sparkling water. I solved the problem for them. "Listen! Take her both!"

The Duchess was really nice, and she asked me if I could please come as her guest to the party that evening after the opening for dinner and cocktails. I told her I couldn't, because that night I was having dinner with George and his family, and I didn't want to cancel that, Duchess or no Duchess.

FRIENDS: SECRET SANTA

I met a good friend of mine through George Brett. Larry was raised in the South by a single mother. As a young man, he once was so broke and hungry that he ate breakfast in a restaurant and he didn't have the money to pay for it. The owner of the restaurant came to him and said, "This $20 on the floor — is this yours?"

"Maybe it is."

So he paid for his breakfast with that $20 that the owner gave him from the floor, and he remembered that owner's generosity and sensitivity. When he became successful, the first thing he did was go back to that restaurant, find that owner, and give him a lot of money. Larry reminded him of the $20 that he knew was not his, and ever since that time, he also started giving out $100 bills at Christmas time to random people, dressing as

Santa Claus to disguise himself.

He did this as Kansas City's Secret Santa for many years, and I joined him for seven years before he died. I was an elf first, but I "graduated" to become a Secret Santa with him. He was on Oprah twice and never showed his face. All the local TV stations tried to find out who we were, and they were never able to, because we did not want to reveal our identity. When I'd go out with him, they wouldn't see our faces.

We were affiliated with the Fire Departments and Sheriff's Departments, and the Sheriffs gave us protection as we gave people money. If somebody in the Fire Department knew of a burn victim or a widow, we'd go to that place and give them $500 or $1,000 or $5,000 to get them started again, passing out money to people who needed it. I even got an honorary special deputy's badge. I normally don't break the law, but if I happen to get stopped for a traffic violation, they just let me go when they see my badge. So I'm a special deputy in both Miami County, Kansas, and Jackson County, Missouri.

You should hear the calls from the Sheriff's Department. One year I was passing out $100 bills, and I had the Miami County sheriff, Frank Kelly, with me. Somebody called the Sheriff's Department and said there was a dirty old man passing out $100 bills to kids. They said, "No, he's not. He's with the sheriff. He's for real."

I went to the bank one time to cash a $30,000 check. A new credit manager at that bank told an officer at the bank, "This guy has got to be in the drug business. He can't be giving that money away."

But the officer knew who I was and knew what I was doing. She started to count the money and I said, "Don't count it!" "I have to. It's a rule."

"Listen, I don't care if there's 30, or 28, or 29, because I'm going to give it away anyway! So if you happen to take a few hundred, I don't care either! I don't want to waste my time waiting on you to count it twice."

Jackson County, Missouri, Sheriff Tom Phillips called me one time and said we have a problem with a lady who's really desperate. I went over there, and she told me her story. I gave her $2,000. She just absolutely cried and cried. I got another call from the sheriff about a family with a house that wasn't heated, and they had no money to heat it. So I went there and gave them $2,000.

On Independence Avenue, I went to a grocery store and there was a guy with his legs amputated from the knees down, in his wheelchair, digging into trash cans for food. I gave him $500, and he was crying. He got to the front door of the store and there was a lady who knew him and had $8 she wanted to give him. He said, "No, no, no, keep it!"

Another time, a woman was at a bus stop carrying a plastic bag. "Ma'am, where are you going?" I asked.

"On the bus."

"I know that, but where are you going?"

"On the bus."

That's where she lived from morning until evening, and when the bus got to its last stop, she stayed there all night at the bus stop. So I gave her $300, and I mean she jumped up and down.

I said, "Ma'am, hide it. I don't want anybody to know you have the money."

We had a grandmother with two kids and her car broke down in freezing weather, and they were sitting there crying. I walked by there and said, "What can I do for you, ma'am?"

"Our car broke down and we have no money to fix it. No money to feed these kids."

"Would $500 help?"

In Osawatomie, Kansas, I walked into a store and saw two ladies there. I gave each one of them $100. One of them said, "We thought you were going to be a customer because you're the first one to show up today!"

I'd go to laundromats and give everybody there $100. I'd give everybody in dollar stores $100, all without asking.

One bitterly cold day I got a call from Secret Santa. This young woman was at the bus station on her way from California to visit her dad in Arkansas. The bus had broken down, and they didn't really have warm clothes and her kids were freezing. So Larry called me and said, "I know you have an airplane. Would you take her?"

"Sure. Ask her if she wants the limo to take her and her kids, or the private airplane. Either way, I'd be glad to do it."

He called me back and said she'd rather take the limo there. So I went down and picked her up, Peggy made them sandwiches and got the kids toys, and they took off in the limo to Arkansas.

Before they got to her town in Arkansas, she called her dad and said, "I'm going to be there in an hour or two." And her dad said, "Don't come to the house. Just meet me at the Wal-Mart."

"Why? I know where the house is."

"No, I want you to come and meet me at Wal-Mart."

When they met at Wal-Mart, he told her that their house had burned down. My driver told me this story, so Secret Santa and I sent her dad $1,000 through the fire department. So they all stayed at her aunt's and it became a good Christmas trip instead of a devastating one. We bought her a plane trip back home from Arkansas to California.

Through Secret Santa, I was awarded lifetime membership on the crime commission in Kansas City, and I donated $5,000 to the Kansas City Police Department. Now this Secret Santa movement is in many major cities in the United States because of Larry, and there are lots more Secret Santa stories. To this day I honor him by carrying $100 bills in my pocket and giving them to people in need.

FRIENDS: DANNY THOMAS

I met Danny Thomas when I was on the board of directors at St. Jude's Hospital in charge of the Midwest area. Danny called me and asked me if I could go to Lebanon with a group of businessmen of Lebanese descent as guests of the Lebanese president. We had dinner with the president at his palace, and we had several functions there with Danny. Although I didn't stay with him as much as I did the prime minister's son, it was an honor to go with him.

When Danny was doing shows in various cities in America, he'd call me and say, "I want you and Peggy to come because all these people as old as I am go to sleep early, but you and Peggy don't have to." We wouldn't go to bed after his shows until 3:00!

Danny was a great guy and we'd talk every two weeks or more. He was always funny and entertaining. We were in Vegas at the Sands and this guy at the next table kept talking about how much he knows Danny and how he's such a good friend of his, but I didn't say anything. In the middle of the show, Danny stopped and said, "I want you to meet a good friend of mine." This guy thought it was him and he was ready to receive some big applause and acknowledgment. But Danny said, "Nabil, would you stand up?"

Later on, Marlo Thomas took over for her dad. When she came to Kansas City I picked her up in my gold Rolls Royce and checked her into the Presidential Suite at the Alameda Plaza Hotel. There was a security guard at her door and anyone – even St. Jude's board members – couldn't get in to see her until the guard cleared it with me. She was fun to be around just like her dad.

FRIENDS: WAYNE NEWTON

Peggy and I also became very good friends
with Wayne Newton. One time Peggy and I
went to Vegas, and we were at Wayne's house
drinking champagne and eating shrimp.
Peggy kept getting these phone calls from
our daughter, Samia. Finally Wayne asked,
"What's going on?"

"Samia's English horse fell over backwards
and hit his head," Peggy said.

The horse was taken to the equine hospital at
Kansas State University to get checked, but
they couldn't help him. They said he would go
blind and his competitive days as a show horse
were over. But Wayne said, "Don't worry. I
have a horse for her."

Wayne sent us Agra, a quick, beautiful white
horse as a gift. And when Samia got that
horse, she won everything.

When we were walking around the compound that same trip, there happened to be people from a television show there doing a story on Wayne. They were there all day, and we kept walking around from place to place. Finally these TV people asked, "Who are you guys?"

"They're friends from Kansas City," Wayne told them.

"Oh! Kansas City! We love Winstead's in Kansas City."

"Well, this guy owns Winstead's!"

They freaked out.

When he'd come to Kansas City to do a show, Wayne would always introduce me from the stage. Peggy and I are the only ones, or George Brett when he was once with us, who would be invited to go back stage to visit with him. One Christmas he sent us a pair of black swans —

he had many exotic birds at his compound in Las Vegas.

FRIENDS: RICKY SKAGGS

Ricky Skaggs is another musician who's a friend of ours. When Ricky came to Kansas City, he'd drop by my office because a country radio station was on the sixth floor of my building. Sometimes if I wasn't there he'd call me and start talking with his Southern accent, and I'd finally have to tell him, "Ricky, speak English!"

One time he came and spent three days at the farm with us at our house. Ricky's a good friend, but I don't know a single song he sings. We've been to a couple of his shows, but I'm not too interested in his singing. These people are my friends not because of how they sing, but because of our relationship with God together.

Most recently, he was touring with the pianist Bruce Hornsby. I happen to know Bruce Hornsby's manager and was able to get four tickets to the concert and a couple of backstage passes. Knowing that the worship pastor at my church is a big Bruce Hornsby fan, I invited him and his wife to join Peggy and me for the concert. Afterwards, Peggy stood in the line to buy some CDs, and I took Randy to the dressing room where he had a 15 minute conversation with Bruce. When Ricky came out to sign autographs for the people buying CDs, he spotted Peggy and greeted her with a great big hug. Finally the security people came and got him because the line was getting longer.

FRIENDS: JON MARTIN

Jon Martin was the tour manager for the promoter of all the big concerts at Kemper Arena during our catering days.

"Hi Jon, how are you?" I asked him before one of the shows.

"Oh man, I have a huge headache."

"Well let me pray for you, and maybe the God of Israel will cure your headache."

We headed down a hallway, and there in the doorway was a truck with the name "Israel Transfer" on it. "You mean Israel Transfer?"

"No," I said. "I mean the God of Israel." So I prayed for him, his headache went away, and he was really taken aback.

Jon later moved to Virginia, and we didn't see him for years. He was a rough-and-tumble, demanding guy who liked to use colorful language. I know it had been 15 years since we'd seen him. One day, Peggy was in the lobby of the church on Sunday morning, just hanging out there waiting. And behind her, somebody said her name. She turned around and here's this man who we wouldn't have recognized, except Peggy recognized his voice. It was Jon Martin.

In the years he had lived in Virginia, he had met an evangelist and gotten saved and been discipled by this guy. He had moved back to Kansas City, and when he knew he was coming back, he started asking friends about churches in Kansas City. There was someone who was a previous member of Christ Community Church who had moved there and said that he should check out Christ Community. So he came, and he started hearing people talk about us. When I prayed for him at Kemper, he thought it was a joke. But now, he knew better. Sometimes you plant seeds that you don't know about until later.

FRIENDS: DAVID GRAHEK

David Grahek and I became good friends
on the ship, The Julius Caesar (from Naples
to New York), in 1959. On the ship we'd beat
each other at ping-pong, and when they had a
buffet for the first class passengers, David and
I would sneak in at midnight and pretend to
be in first class so we could eat at the buffet.

David's father was a genius inventor. He
invented a golf cart that would electronically
walk behind you, and a remote control for the
yacht he kept on Chesapeake Bay. When I was
visiting in Lancaster before school started at
Fort Collins, I remember his father putting
together the golf carts while we were there.
To this day, David is one of my best friends.
He's the guy who taught me how to play golf,
the guy who fixed me up with a blind date,
and for 20 years we used to meet each year in
Myrtle Beach with 20 other guys to play golf
for four or five days. And every once in a while
David would make the trip to Kansas City to
play a few rounds.

AFTERWORD

Do you agree? Wild and wonderful,
slightly wacky, definitely entertaining, no?

You can see pictures at Nabil's website:
www.nabilhaddad38.com.

Want to arrange an event to hear the stories
in person?

Write to Nabil at:
Louisburg Press
P.O. Box 4
Cleveland, MO 64734

or email:
nabilhaddad38@yahoo.com

Made in the USA
Columbia, SC
05 January 2023

75575250R00098